SCIENTISTS AT WORK

Into the Fire
VOLCANOLOGISTS

Paul Mason

Heinemann Library
Chicago, Illinois

Customer Service 888-454-2279
Visit our Web site at www.heinemannraintree.com

Design: Richard Parker and Manhattan Design
Illustrations: Darren Lingard
Picture Research: Mica Brancic and Virginia Stroud-Lewis
Production: Alison Parsons

Originated by Modern Age
Printed and bound in China by Leo Paper Group

12 11 10 09 08
10 9 8 7 6 5 4 3 2 1

Library of Congress Cataloging-in-Publication Data

Mason, Paul.
  Into the fire : volcanologists / Paul Mason. -- 1st ed.
    p. cm. -- (Scientists at work)
  Includes bibliographical references and index.
  ISBN 978-1-403-49950-9 (hardback : alk. paper) -- ISBN 978-1-403-49957-8 (pbk. : alk. paper) 1. Volcanologists--Juvenile literature. I. Title.
  QE521.3.M384 2007
  551.21092--dc22
                        2007012492

Acknowledgments

The publishers would like to thank the following for permission to reproduce photographs: ©Alamy pp. **15** (Photo Resource Hawaii), **26** (Gary Cook); ©Corbis pp. **5**, **20** (Roger Ressmeyer), **9** (James L. Amos), **14** (Stuart Westmorland); ©Empics p. **24**; ©Getty Images pp. **27**, **21** (AFP); ©PhotoLibrary.com p. **13** (PhotoDisc/StockTrek); ©Reuters p. **10** (Sigit Pamungkas); © US Geological Survey pp. **4**, **7**, **16**, **18**, **19**, **22**, **23**, **25**, **11** (Jeremy Bishop), **12** Wesley Bocxe, **17** (Zephyr).

Cover photograph of Mount Etna reproduced with permission of ©Getty Images/Photonica/David Trood.

The publishers would like to thank Tom Simkin for his assistance in the preparation of this book.

Every effort has been made to contact copyright holders of any material reproduced in this book. Any omissions will be rectified in subsequent printings if notice is given to the publishers.

Disclaimer

Contents

Any words appearing in the text in bold, **like this**, are explained in the Glossary.

What Is a Volcanologist?

A volcanologist is a person who studies volcanoes. A volcano is a large opening in the surface of the Earth. The opening lets out hot rock and other material. One day a volcanologist might stand next to a stream of **lava** and measure its temperature. The next day he or she might be taking notes while watching a volcano erupt. A lot of the work is research done in offices and libraries. It is an exciting and interesting job.

What did early people think of volcanoes?

In the past, some people thought that when a volcano erupted, it was the work of the gods. They believed the eruption occurred because the gods were angry. Other people believed that volcanoes were the homes of the gods.

Volcanologists spend a lot of their time in offices doing research. But, they also do **fieldwork**. This can mean visiting some very dangerous places.

The first volcanologists were ancient Romans. The Romans did not know how volcanoes were formed or erupted. Despite this, they made the first accurate recordings of volcanic eruptions. Watching and recording what happens is an important part of a volcanologist's job.

Volcanologists today

Today, volcanologists do not just record volcanic activity. They also act as detectives and historians, figuring out how volcanoes will behave in the future. They use physics, chemistry, and mathematics to investigate how volcanoes work.

This farmer lives in the shadow of Mount Etna, a volcano in Italy. The fertile soil on the volcano's slopes makes it worth the farmer's risk.

The science behind it: Volcanoes

A volcano is a large opening in the Earth's surface. It is created as hot rock forces its way to the surface. Volcanoes come in different shapes and sizes: the most familiar is a cone shape, with a huge well called a **crater** at the top.

What Do Volcanologists Study?

Volcanologists try to determine how volcanoes work. They figure out how volcanoes **erupt**, study the different things that come out of them, and even hope to **predict** when eruptions will happen.

Where volcanologists study

Volcanologists study the places where there is volcanic activity. Most volcanoes form at the edges of **tectonic plates**. Tectonic plates are parts of the Earth's **crust**, which is its hard outer shell. This crust is broken up into pieces called plates.

Volcanoes form when hot rock underneath the Earth's crust finds its way up to the surface. Most volcanoes that can be seen on land are formed where one plate sinks below another.

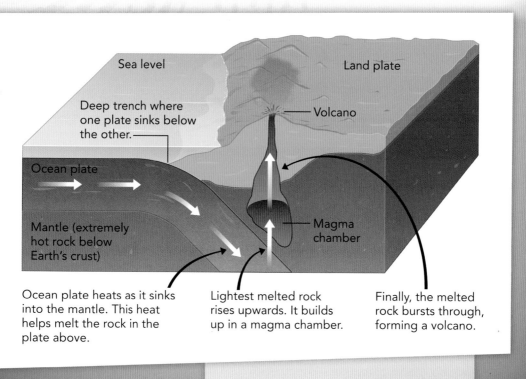

Sea level

Land plate

Deep trench where one plate sinks below the other.

Volcano

Ocean plate

Mantle (extremely hot rock below Earth's crust)

Magma chamber

Ocean plate heats as it sinks into the mantle. This heat helps melt the rock in the plate above.

Lightest melted rock rises upwards. It builds up in a magma chamber.

Finally, the melted rock bursts through, forming a volcano.

Volcanoes are common where one tectonic plate sinks below another.

Earthquakes and volcanoes

Like volcanoes, small earthquakes are common at the edges of tectonic plates. They occur as one tectonic plate sinks underneath another. The rock in the plate underneath melts as it sinks into the Earth. When molten rock moves to the surface, it can cause earthquakes that sometimes lead to eruptions. Because of this, volcanologists are also interested in earthquakes.

The bright red dots on this image of the Earth show the locations of major earthquakes. The yellow lines show tectonic plate boundaries. This zone is known as the Ring of Fire.

The science behind it: Big earthquakes

Big earthquakes occur when the edges of two plates want to move in different directions, but are held tight against each other. Eventually, the stress becomes too great. The plates suddenly move, causing the ground to shiver and shake.

What types of eruptions do volcanologists study?

The biggest events a volcanologist studies are giant eruptions. The effects of these can spread around the world. When the island of Krakatau erupted in 1883, most of the island was blown apart by the eruption. The noise was so loud that it was heard thousands of miles away.

When Mount Pinatubo in the Philippine Islands erupted in June 1991, it sent huge clouds of ash into the air. These clouds spread so far that they could be seen from space. The ash resembled a ring of cloud around the world.

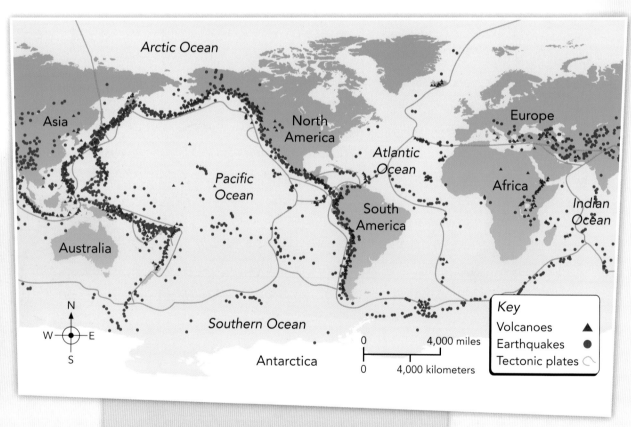

Volcanoes and earthquake zones around the world. The Pacific Ring of Fire circles the Pacific Ocean.

Smaller volcanic events

Most volcanic eruptions are much smaller than Krakatau or Mount Pinatubo. The small volcanic events a volcanologist might study include:
- a small stream of lava running down a hillside
- smoke or gases coming from a volcano
- minor earthquakes
- **hot springs** and **geysers**, which are influenced by heat deep underground, just as volcanoes are.

Volcanologists study all of these small events. Sometimes, these small events provide clues about when a big eruption is about to occur.

Undersea volcanoes

More volcanic eruptions happen under the sea than on land. Of course, nobody sees these eruptions. Many happen in the deep ocean, but others are very close to shore. Volcanologists are able to study the effects of volcanic activity using diving gear and other specialized equipment.

Volcanologists take temperature measurements and samples of water from Old Faithful, a geyser in Wyoming. The geyser is so famous that it even has its own webcam for people who want to watch its eruptions online.

The science behind it: The Ring of Fire

The Ring of Fire sits around the edges of the Pacific Ocean. It gets its name from the high number of volcanoes there. This is where most of the world's volcanoes are located. So, of course, it's also where many volcanologists do fieldwork.

What Is It Like To Be a Volcanologist?

Being a volcanologist can be exciting, especially when working in the field. But volcanoes can be dangerous and unpredictable, even for experts. Although the job can be risky, relatively few volcanologists are killed doing their work.

Gathering information

Volcanologists sometimes spend years observing and recording the activity of a volcano. They collect information about everything that has happened at the volcano. This is done in the form of notes, sketches, measurements, photographs, and other information. Different volcanologists add material about the areas they specialize in studying.

Volcanologists record small eruptions, escapes of gas, what type of gas the volcano is producing, temperature of lava flows, earthquakes, and other events. Sometimes, it is only clear later whether or not an event or measurement was important.

Working close to a volcano can be unpredictable and even dangerous.

Analyzing information

Volcanologists spend a lot of time working indoors, analyzing the information they have gathered. They look for changes in the way a volcano behaves. For example, a volcano might start to produce different gases or the temperature or type of lava might change. These changes mean something is happening deep underground and may signal that an eruption is about to occur.

Fieldwork

Most volcanologists also spend time doing fieldwork. They visit the volcanoes they are studying. They measure the ground to see if it has moved slightly. Some volcanologists collect specimens from recent eruptions, so that they can analyze them in their laboratories. Others study ancient volcanoes in hopes of discovering how they erupted.

This man is wearing breathing equipment to avoid poisonous gases.

TOOLS OF THE TRADE: PORTABLE SEISMOMETER

A portable **seismometer** is a machine for measuring tiny movements in the Earth. This is an important tool for a volcanologist. It can measure the strength of earth tremors at or near volcanoes, which gives the volcanologist clues about what is happening deep underground.

The most explosive volcanic eruptions are graded 8 on the Volcanic Explosivity Index (VEI). Their ash cloud reaches at least 30 miles (50 kilometers) into the air. This photo shows the VEI 3-4 eruption of Mexico's Mount Popocatepetl volcano in 2000.

Witnessing a big eruption

Volcanologists keep a close watch on **active volcanoes**. They hope to be able to predict when a large eruption will occur. A large eruption can cause death and destroy anything in its path.

Many volcanologists want to see a large eruption if it happens. They hope to gather information that will help save lives in the future. If volcanologists can get better at predicting when and how a volcano is going to erupt, it will give more people more time to be **evacuated** to safer areas.

The Volcanic Explosivity Index

Volcanologists measure the size of a volcanic eruption using the Volcanic Explosivity Index (VEI). They measure the amount of lava, ash, and other material the volcano spews out. They look at the height of its ash cloud and then decide how the eruption should be described. These descriptions range from "gentle" to "mega-colossal."

The VEI gives eruptions a score ranging from zero to eight. Each number represents an increase of ten times. So a volcano scoring five is ten times as big as a volcano scoring four.

More than 800 people were killed when Mount Pinatubo in the Philippines erupted in 1991. It was the 20th century's most powerful volcanic eruption.

The science behind it: Volcanoes and weather

Large volcanic eruptions can have a major effect on the world's weather. The large clouds of ash they throw into the air prevent the sun's heat from getting through. For example, after the 1815 eruption of Tambora in Indonesia, the next summer was the coldest summer the world had ever experienced. Some places that were normally warm had snow on the ground in the middle of summer.

Working in the deep sea

Many volcanic eruptions happen deep under the sea. Volcanologists can use an undersea vehicle called a **submersible** (see box) to look at what is happening at the bottom of the deep oceans. The submersible is sent down and then sends information back to the surface. At the surface, scientists are able to analyze what the information means.

This submersible is about to make its voyage into the deep ocean.

TOOLS OF THE TRADE: THE SUBMERSIBLE

A submersible is a vehicle for journeying deep underwater. Volcanologists sometimes use them to investigate undersea volcanoes. Submersibles are specially designed to survive the great **pressure** deep underwater. Some are piloted, but in the deepest oceans they are radio-controlled from the surface. They send images and other scientific information to the volcanologists on the surface.

Spectacular lava flows into the sea, creating a steaming, hissing landscape where the land meets the ocean in Hawaii.

There are more volcanoes under the sea than there are above the ground.

Undersea volcanoes are among the most spectacular of all. The Hawaiian Islands, for example, were created by a volcanic hot spot far below on the seabed. The islands are just the tips of the volcanoes this hot spot formed. If the ocean was drained away, they would be the tallest mountains in the world, at more than 33,000 feet (10,000 meters).

Paperwork

Many volcanologists work for universities. They are able to travel to research volcanoes and may be based near volcanic activity. Usually, part of their time is spent grading student papers, teaching classes, and giving lectures.

What Happens When a Mountain Explodes?

At 8:32 a.m. on May 18, 1980, volcanologists proved just how useful they can be. It was the day Mount St. Helens in Washington erupted.

Sleeping giant

Mount St. Helens was a **dormant**, or sleeping, volcano. There had been no large volcanic eruptions there since 1857. The last very large eruption had been in 1800.

Volcanologists first knew something unusual was happening on March 20, 1980. An earthquake measuring 4.2 on the **Richter Scale** occurred under the volcano. A week later, there was a small eruption near the **summit**. Then, steam began to appear from cracks in the ground.

Harmonic tremors

Harmonic tremors are a type of continuous earthquake. They have regular rises and falls in the amount of quaking. Volcanologists know that harmonic tremors are a sign that **magma**, the **molten** rock beneath the Earth's crust, is moving underground. On April 1, harmonic tremors were detected under Mount St. Helens.

The bulge in the side of Mount St. Helens was caused by a build-up of magma high up inside the volcano.

Evacuation

By late April, the side of the mountain was bulging out. Almost every day there were small explosions of ash and rock on the volcano. People living nearby were evacuated from their homes for safety.

During the first half of May, the bulge grew at a rate of 5 feet (1.5 meters) each day. Everyone thought an eruption was coming, but nobody knew when or how big it would be.

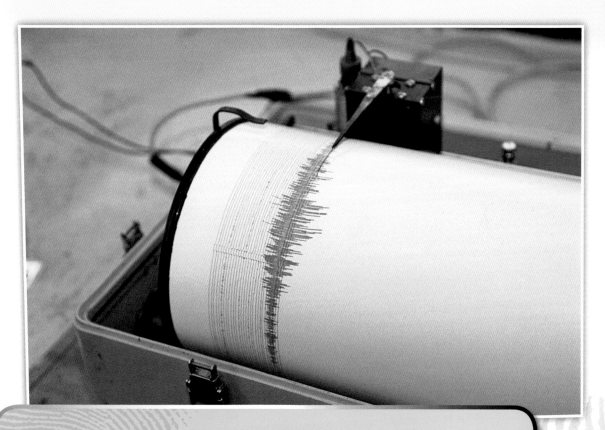

TOOLS OF THE TRADE: MEASURING TREMORS

Tremors are measured with a **seismograph**. This is a recording of the Earth's movements on a piece of paper produced by a seismometer (see box on page 11). The seismograph shows tremors as a jagged line on a piece of paper. The bigger the spike on the line, the bigger the tremor or earthquake.

The U.S. Geological Survey

The **U.S. Geological Survey (USGS)** is a government organization that investigates physical geography. One of the things it investigates is volcanic activity. The USGS had a lookout post just 5 miles (8 kilometers) from Mount St. Helens. The volcanologist on duty on May 18 was David Johnston.

Mount St. Helens erupts

At 8:32 a.m., Johnston radioed his base in the city of Vancouver: "Vancouver! Vancouver! This is it!" The eruption had finally begun.

The eruption had been triggered by an earthquake measuring 5.1 on the Richter Scale. The earthquake moved the bulge on the side of the mountain. Much of the north face of the mountain was swept away in a landslide. The gas, steam, and magma beneath the volcano burst out, similar to soda from a shaken-up bottle. Then, a huge cloud of ash poured out of the volcano. It eventually reached 16 miles (27 kilometers) into the atmosphere.

Within 3.5 hours of the eruption of Mount St. Helens, ash had spread as far as Idaho, hundreds of miles away.

Results of the eruption

The results of the eruption were far-reaching:
- 57 people and thousands of animals died.
- The height of the mountain was reduced by 1,300 feet (400 meters).
- An area of 230 miles^2 (600 km^2) of forest was flattened by the blast.

Why did Mount St. Helens erupt?

Mount St. Helens erupted because an underground chamber, or store, of magma was disturbed. It had grown slowly but steadily below the mountain, until the magma forced its way to the surface.

David Johnston was the volcanologist killed when Mount St. Helens erupted.

WHO'S WHO: David Johnston

David Johnston was the volcanologist on duty when Mount St. Helens erupted. He was one of the only volcanologists to predict that an explosion would be sideways, rather than upward. Johnston was killed when the volcano did explode sideways. The ridge from which he had been watching has been named Johnston Ridge in his honor.

Why Is Volcanology Useful?

Volcanology is useful because it helps us to know more about how volcanoes behave. The world's population gets bigger every year. As it grows, more and more people are living close to volcanoes. Volcanic eruptions have killed hundreds of thousands of people in the past. Knowing what might happen when a volcano erupts helps us to plan how to keep people safer.

Killer volcanoes

The size of a volcanic eruption can be measured by the amount of ash the volcano produces. The number of people killed depends on the size of the eruption, how many people are living near the volcano when it erupts, and how well prepared they are for the eruption.

Even when volcanoes don't kill, they can still ruin thousands of lives. This is the aftermath of a mud flow in the Philippines. Mud flows destroy buildings and bury fields, making life almost impossible for local people.

These are seven of the biggest known volcanic eruptions:

Size of volcano by approximate death toll:

1   1815: Tambora, Indonesia—70,000+ killed
2   1883: Krakatau, Indonesia—36,000+ killed
3   1902: Pelée, Martinique—26,000+ killed
4   1985: Nevado del Ruiz, Colombia—23,000+ killed
5   79 CE: Vesuvius, Italy—18,000+ killed

Size of volcano by ash volume:

1   1815: Tambora, Indonesia—50 miles^3 (80 km^3) of ash
2   1883: Krakatau, Indonesia—11 miles^3 (18 km^3) of ash
3   1912: Katmai, United States—7.5 miles^3 (12 km^3) of ash
4   1991: Pinatubo, Philippines—4 miles^3 (7 km^3) of ash
5   79 CE: Vesuvius, Italy—2 miles^3 (3 km^3) of ash

The table shows that the most powerful volcanoes do not always kill the most people. The eruption of Pelée killed tens of thousands because so many people lived near the volcano. Katmai was a more powerful eruption but killed fewer people because fewer people lived nearby.

An injured woman is helped to safety by a soldier and a rescue worker, after the eruption of the Nevado del Ruiz volcano in Colombia. The 1985 eruption killed at least 23,000 people.

WHO'S WHO: Giuseppe Mercalli

Giuseppe Mercalli (1850–1914) was a famous Italian volcanologist who invented the Mercalli Scale for measuring the damaging effects of earthquakes. His detailed descriptions of the eruptions of Stromboli and Vulcano provided useful material for volcanologists around the world.

Which are today's most dangerous volcanoes?

The most dangerous volcanoes today are the ones that have the most people living near them. When Vesuvius in Italy erupted in 79 CE, it killed at least 18,000 people. Today, some volcanologists think that in the first 15 minutes after another big eruption, the area up to 4 miles (7 kilometers) from the volcano could be destroyed. More than 1 million people now live this close to Vesuvius.

Mauna Loa in Hawaii is a Decade Volcano (see box). The city of Hilo, with a population of more than 40,000, is built partly on the hardened lava flow of Mauna Loa's previous eruptions.

The science behind it: Decade Volcanoes

Sixteen volcanoes around the world have been named Decade Volcanoes. They are believed to be especially dangerous because:

- Many people live near them.
- They could have a major eruption.

The Decade Volcanoes that appear in this book include Mauna Loa in Hawaii, as well as Vesuvius in Italy.

Before new buildings are allowed near Mount Rainier in Washington, scientists must decide if they would be at risk from the volcano.

Knowing how a volcano might behave can help the people who live nearby prepare for an eruption. Volcanologists can help make plans before an eruption happens. Based on volcanologists' knowledge of how volcanoes have behaved in the past, they can give possible answers to questions like:

- Are there likely to be lava flows? Which direction will they go?
- Is there danger from a landslide or mud flow?
- Could there be a giant cloud of ash?
- How big of an area might be affected by an eruption?

After listening to the advice of volcanologists, the government might decide that it is a bad idea to build homes in a specific area. Volcanologists also help by warning people when they think an eruption might be coming. This gives those in danger time to leave.

When eruptions occur

Volcanologists can sometimes help prevent a disaster from happening. One example is when Mount Etna in Italy began to erupt in 1991. Lava began to flow toward the town of Zafferana. Barriers were built in its way, but the lava could not be **diverted**. Volcanologists then decided to drop large blocks of concrete into one of the volcano's lava tubes, the place where lava comes out from the volcano. The blocks worked as hoped and the lava flow stopped before it reached Zafferana.

Today, roughly 3 million people live around Italy's Mount Vesuvius. An evacuation plan has been developed in case the volcano erupts again.

Can volcanologists predict eruptions?

Volcanologists know that when some of the smaller-scale volcanic events happen together, an eruption may be coming. These include:

- Earth tremors
- swelling of the volcano surface
- changes in the amount or type of gas being released
- harmonic vibrations.

There are also other warnings that a serious eruption is coming. But the occurrence of these things does not always lead to a serious eruption. No one is ever exactly sure when and how a volcano is about to erupt. Despite all of their research, volcanologists can still sometimes be taken by surprise.

The 1980 eruption of Mount St. Helens in Washington showed that volcanologists do not always make accurate predictions. Few expected the eruption to be as large as it was.

TRICKS OF THE TRADE: UNZEN DRILLING PROJECT

Mount Unzen in Japan is one of the world's most dangerous volcanoes. Volcanologists have drilled a hole in the volcano to find out more about how it works. The hole reaches almost 1.2 miles (2 kilometers) inside the volcano. Scientists hope to discover why eruptions often occur in the same places on the volcano.

How Do You Become a Volcanologist?

In the past, many volcanologists were wealthy people who could afford to spend their time studying volcanoes. Others were government officials. These early volcanologists began to understand how volcanoes worked. They even had some ideas about when volcanoes might erupt.

The work of early volcanologists made people realize how important it was to understand as much as possible about volcanoes. By the 1800s, it had become possible to earn a living studying volcanic activity.

Tourists on a guided visit at the edge of the crater of Villarrica Volcano in Chile.

University studies

Most volcanologists begin their careers by going to college. They often study geography or **geology**. Universities sometimes offer courses in which students combine classroom study with fieldwork.

After they have finished classes, some volcanologists decide to take even more courses on subjects dealing with volcanology. Some will go on to work for an organization, such as the U.S. Geological Survey.

Film and photography work

A few volcanologists make money by filming and photographing volcanic eruptions. This can be very exciting work—you have to be ready to leave at a moment's notice if an eruption is happening somewhere. But it is dangerous work, too. The most famous volcano filmmakers, Katia and Maurice Krafft, were killed by an ash flow in 1991.

Becoming a volcanologist involves a combination of classroom study and hands-on experience of volcanoes.

WHO'S WHO: Masao Mimatsu

Masao Mimatsu (1888–1977) was a Japanese postal worker and an amateur volcanologist. He recorded the daily changes in the volcanic growth of the Showa-Shinzan Mountain, a volcano that first appeared in a cornfield in Japan in 1944. In 1946 Mimatsu used his life savings to buy the volcano. When he appeared at the World Volcano Conference in 1948, his work was widely praised.

Volcanic History

1620 BCE:
Santorini, Greece:
Volcanic eruptions blow
the island of Santorini
apart, then bury it under
100 ft (30 m) of **pumice**

79 CE:
Mt. Vesuvius, Italy:
The eruption of Mt.
Vesuvius buries the
cities of Pompeii and
Herculaneum, killing
an estimated
18,000 people

1792:
Mt. Unzen, Kyushu
Island, Japan:
The collapse of an old
lava dome during the
eruption of Mt. Unzen
causes an avalanche. A
tsunami is also caused
by the underground
activity. In the end,
an estimated 15,000
people are killed, most
by the tsunami.

1883:
Krakatau, Dutch
East Indies:
The eruption of
Krakatau destroys
two-thirds of the
island and causes
a tsunami that hits
Java and Sumatra,
killing at least
36,000 people

1600–1000BCE   0–100CE   1700s   1800s

1500 BCE:
Etna, Italy:
Etna is Europe's
largest volcano, and
this is the first
volcanic eruption
that people keep
records of (though
many others had
happened before)

1783:
Laki volcano, Iceland:
The eruption of Laki
lasts from June of 1783
through February of
1784. Thick clouds from
the eruption kill the
island's livestock and
crops. More than 9,000
people die, mostly due
to lack of food.

1815:
Mt. Tambora, Dutch East Indies
(now Sumbawa, Indonesia):
The eruption of Tambora is the
largest volcanic eruption in
modern history. At least 70,000
people are killed. Roughly 10,000
die as a result of explosions
and fallen ash. At least 60,000
die from lack of food. The effects
of the eruption are felt around
the world.

1963:
Surtsey, Iceland:
Undersea volcanic activity results in the creation of a completely new island, Surtsey, off the coast of Iceland

1985:
Nevado del Ruiz, Colombia:
The eruption of Nevada del Ruiz causes mudslides that bury most of the town of Armero and almost ruin Chinchiná. An estimated 23,000 people die as a result.

1997:
Soufrière Hills volcano, Montserrat:
The Soufrière Hills volcano had been erupting since July 1995. A major eruption on June 25, 1997, kills 20 people and makes the southern two-thirds of Montserrat uninhabitable. Roughly 8,000 of the 12,000 people who lived on the island are forced to leave the island and move elsewhere.

1900s

2000s ≫

1980:
Mt. St. Helens, Washington:
One of the most famous volcanic eruptions of modern times shows that when the side of a volcano collapses, it can set off explosive eruptions

1991:
Kilauea, Hawaii:
Kilauea spews out large lava flows. The lava buries 8 miles (13 kilometers) of roads, 181 homes, and a tourist center.

Mt. Pinatubo, Luzon Island, Philippines:
The eruption of Mt. Pinatubo buries more than 300 miles^2 (780 km^2) under volcanic ash and results in more than 800 deaths. It is the most powerful volcanic eruption of the 20th century.

1902:
Mt. Pelée, Martinique, West Indies:
On May 8, Mt. Pelée erupts. The city of St. Pierre is destroyed, and at least 26,000 people are killed.

2002:
Mt. Nyiragongo, Democratic Republic of Congo:
The town of Goma is partially destroyed by lava flows from the volcano. Roughly 500,000 people are forced to leave their homes.

Glossary

active volcano volcano that has regular volcanic activity

crater funnel-shaped depression in the ground, usually caused by volcanic activity. Many cone-shaped volcanoes have a crater at the top, some of them can be very large.

crust hard outer layer of the Earth

diverted sent in a new, different direction

dormant asleep. When people speak of a dormant volcano, they mean one that has not erupted for a very long time.

erupt explosive release of lava and other materials from a volcano

evacuated taken to a place of greater safety

fieldwork work that is done in the natural environment. For a volcanologist this might be the site of a volcano.

geology study of the Earth's structure, especially its rocks

geyser hole in the Earth's surface that shoots a spout of water into the air, often at regular intervals

hot spring place where water that has been heated by volcanic activity finds its way to the surface. Some hot springs are cool enough to bathe in, but others are so hot you cannot touch the water.

lava melted rock, or magma, that has found a way through the Earth's crust and into the air

magma super hot, liquid rock beneath the Earth's surface

molten melted

predict tell what will happen in the future. Volcanologists try to predict when and how volcanoes might erupt.

pressure force that pushes on something

pumice lightweight rock with holes in it, made when lava cools down and hardens

Richter Scale scale for measuring the power of earthquakes

seismograph recording device showing Earth's movements, produced by a seismometer

seismometer machine for measuring the strength of movements in the Earth

submersible specially designed vehicle for exploring deep under the ocean. Some submersibles are driven by humans, while others use remote control.

summit top

tectonic plates areas of the Earth's crust. The crust is made up of many different plates, each of them touching the ones next to them.

tsunami giant wave caused by an under-sea earthquake

U.S. Geological Survey (USGS) science organization that studies the landscape, our natural resources, and the natural hazards that threaten us

Find Out More

Further reading

Colson, Mary. *Turbulent Planet: Earth Erupts—Volcanoes*. Chicago: Raintree, 2004.

Greenwood, Rosie. *I Wonder Why Volcanoes Blow Their Tops And Other Questions About Natural Disasters*. Boston: Kingfisher Books, 2004.

Magloff, Lisa. *Eye Wonder: Volcano*. New York: Dorling Kindersley, 2003.

Shone, Rob. *Volcanoes*. New York: Rosen Publishing, 2007.

Waldron, Melanie. *Mapping Earthforms: Volcanoes*. Chicago: Heinemann Library, 2007.

Webster, Christine. *Mauna Loa*. New York: Weigl Publishers, Inc., 2003.

Websites

The U.S. Geological Survey's website provides numerous links to various volcano-related websites:
http://www.usgs.gov/science/science.php?term=1209&type=feature

To see a list of the Decade Volcanoes visit:
http://vulcan.wr.usgs.gov/Volcanoes/DecadeVolcanoes/framework.html

Part of the Savage Earth television series, the Out of the Inferno: Volcanoes television show and website offers detailed information and movie clips on volcanoes:
http://www.pbs.org/wnet/savageearth

Visit this website to see more exciting movie clips of volcanoes:
http://volcano.und.edu/vwdocs/movies/movie.html

Read questions and answers about volcanoes at:
http://volcano.und.edu/vwdocs/ask_a.html

Index